# WAITING FOR NOËL

*An Advent Story*

*Written by* ANN DIXON

*Illustrated by* MARK GRAHAM

EERDMANS BOOKS FOR YOUNG READERS

GRAND RAPIDS, MICHIGAN / CAMBRIDGE, U. K.

Text ©1996 by Ann Dixon
Illustrations copyright ©1996 by Mark Graham
Published 2000 by Eerdmans Books for Young Readers
An imprint of Wm. B. Eerdmans Publishing Company
255 Jefferson S.E., Grand Rapids, Michigan 49503
P.O. Box 163, Cambridge  CB3 9PU  U.K.

00 01 02 03 04 05     6 5 4 3 2 1

Library of Congress Cataloging-in-Publication Data
Dixon, Ann
Waiting for Noël : An Advent story / written by Ann Dixon;
illustrated by Mark Graham.
p. cm.
Previously issued as Merry birthday, Nora Noël.
Summary: Noël's father tells her the story of how the whole family looked
forward to her arrival and how they celebrated her birth as their own Christmas baby.
ISBN 0-8028-5192-4 (cloth : alk. paper)
[1. Babies—Fiction. 2. Birthdays—Fiction. 3. Christmas—Fiction.] I. Graham, Mark,
1950–ill. II. Dixon, Ann.  III. Title.
PZ7.D642 Wai 1999
[E]—dc21                 99-023230
CIP

The book was designed by Gayle Brown.

To all Christmas babies, especially the First  — *A.D.*


To Elizabeth and Bunzo — *M.G.*

When the earth

is frozen into stillness and

night creeps upon us at midday

the first Advent candle is lit,

small flame flickering bravely

through December darkness.

With hope for

good things to come,

each year we await the

Christmas babe.

You, too, Noël,

came to us at Christmas,

a baby as helpless and new

as any other.

But our waiting for you

lasted longer than Christmas,

longer than Advent,

longer even than winter.


This Advent story is yours, Noël.

Come sit on my lap,

and I will tell it to you

candle by candle,

season by season.

You began with the spring

as days grew longer,

earth waking into life.

Pussy willows bulged, soft as cat paws.

"Is this spring?" asked James.

"I think so," said Anna.

While we waited and watched,

your mother napped and didn't feel like eating.

"Mama's no fun," complained James.

"Why is she always tired?" asked Anna.

"Be patient," I told them. "Soon, I hope,

we will have good news."

Today

when snowflakes

swarm to earth,

falling headlong

through dusk into darkness,

two Advent candles are lit,

partners in brightening the night.

With peace in our hearts

we look forward to

the Christmas babe.

As for you, Noël,

you brightened even the summer.

By then we knew you really were coming.

Outside in our garden the flowers grew.

Inside, so did you.

So did your mother!

Not in height, but in rosy roundness.

She told us you fluttered like a butterfly

inside her, speaking with gentle wings

the mysterious language of babes.

Your mother understood.

Peacefully she listened

to each message you sent.

*N*ow, when the sun

tucks us in for another

cold, long night with

a blanket of pink and

tangerine dreams,

three Advent candles are lit,

a cheerful crowd

upon the table.

With joy in the season

we prepare for the

Christmas babe.

But you, Noël, brought dreams

we could hold and touch.

Blankets of many colors appeared—

gifts of soft flannel swaddling,

thick, downy quilts,

coverlets knit with joy and pleasure

to cozy our autumn dreams.

We felt and listened and watched

for each bumping, bulging motion.

"Can you hear us?" asked Anna.

"Don't kick Mama!" scolded James

until we laughed and I explained

how you were growing.

Today, when

the sun skims the rim

of a smooth blue sky

and night rises

soft with moonlight,

four Advent candles are lit,

a promise we know

won't be broken.

With faith in the power

of light, we welcome the

Christmas babe.

And you, Noël, kept your promise

spoken in months of flutter, kick, and dream.

On Christmas Eve, we were ready.

Presents waited under the tree for "Baby."

We took turns rocking your cradle,

just for practice.

The table was set, candles lit,
but Mama was restless,
too restless for food.
While we opened packages,
she paced. "Soon," she
assured us, "our baby
will be here."

*N*ow, as night

overtakes the fading sun,

and a Christmas moon

shines clear and full,

five candles are lit,

their blaze reflected in

the stars and our hearts.

With light and love

we give thanks for the

Christmas babe.

Noël, you greeted us on Christmas Day

with a cry of surprise

at a world so vast and unknown.

Mama held you close, heart to heart,

until you understood that love is here.

I murmured my welcome

and stroked your cheek.

You gave a sigh that fluttered through us.

Your eyes opened,

wide and deep as the heavens.

"You're so soft!" whispered Anna,

holding fingers tightly curled.

"You're so little!" said James, standing tall.

"You're our Noël," Mama told you.

We all agreed and gave thanks

for our own Christmas babe.

# A Note about Advent

Advent is a season of preparation celebrated by Christians around the world. The word Advent comes from a Latin verb meaning "to come." For most Christians, Advent begins four Sundays prior to Christmas and culminates on Christmas Day. In the Greek and Russian churches, Advent begins six weeks before Christmas. In this story, the tradition of the Advent wreath, which originated in Germany and Scandinavia, is honored. One candle is lit each Sunday, with the fifth lit on Christmas Day. In the order of lighting, the candles represent hope, peace, joy, faith, and love. Although Advent traditions vary, the reason for observing Advent remains the same: to prepare our hearts for welcoming God's gift of light and love, his son Jesus.